PSALMS POEMS & PRAYERS

COMPILED CARVED AND COMPRESSED BY KREG YINGST

PSALMS POEMS& PRAYERS

a blockbook of praise

KREG YINGST

STARVING ARTIST BOOKS

PSALMS 19, 98, 113, 126, 130, 134, 146, 150 TAKEN FROM THE HOLY BIBLE, NEW INTERNATIONAL VERSION, COPYRIGHT © 1973, 1978, 1984 INTERNATIONAL BIBLE SOCIETY. USED BY PERMISSION OF ZONDERVAN BIBLE PUBLISHERS

ISBN 978-0-6151-9993-1

FOR MY BELOVED

CONTENTS

TEACH ME TO PRAY

ST. JOHN BERCHMANS

LORD, TEACH ME HOW TO PRAY - O LORD, IN MY MEDI-TATION LET A FIRE FLAME OUT OPEN MY LIPS, O LORD AND MY MOUTH WILL DECLARE YOUR PRAISE

2

GLORY BE TO GOD FOR
DAPPLED THINGS —
FOR SKIES OF COUPLE-
COLOUR AS A BRINDED
COW;
FOR ROSE-MOLES ALL
IN STIPPLE UPON
TROUT THAT SWIM;
FRESH-FIRECOAL
CHESTNUT FALLS
FINCHES WINGS;
LANDSCAPES PLOTTED
AND PIECED—FOLD, FALLOW
AND PLOUGH;

AND ALL TRADES,
THEIR GEAR AND
TACKLE AND TRIM
- - - - - - - - - - - - - - -
ALL THINGS COUNTER
ORIGINAL, SPARE,
STRANGE;
WHATEVER IS FICKLE,
FRECKLED (WHO KNOWS
HOW?) WITH SWIFT,
SLOW, SWEET, SOUR;
ADAZZLE, DIM;
HE FATHERS-FORTH
WHOSE BEAUTY IS PAST
CHANGE: PRAISE HIM

SELAH

The heaven's declare the glory of God, and the skies proclaim the work of his hands. Day after day they pour

FORTH SPEECH
NIGHT AFTER
NIGHT THEY
DISPLAY KNOW-
LEDGE. THERE
IS NO SPEECH
OR LANGUAGE
WHERE THEIR
VOICE IS NOT
HEARD. THEIR
VOICE GOES
OUT INTO ALL
THE EARTH,
THEIR WORDS

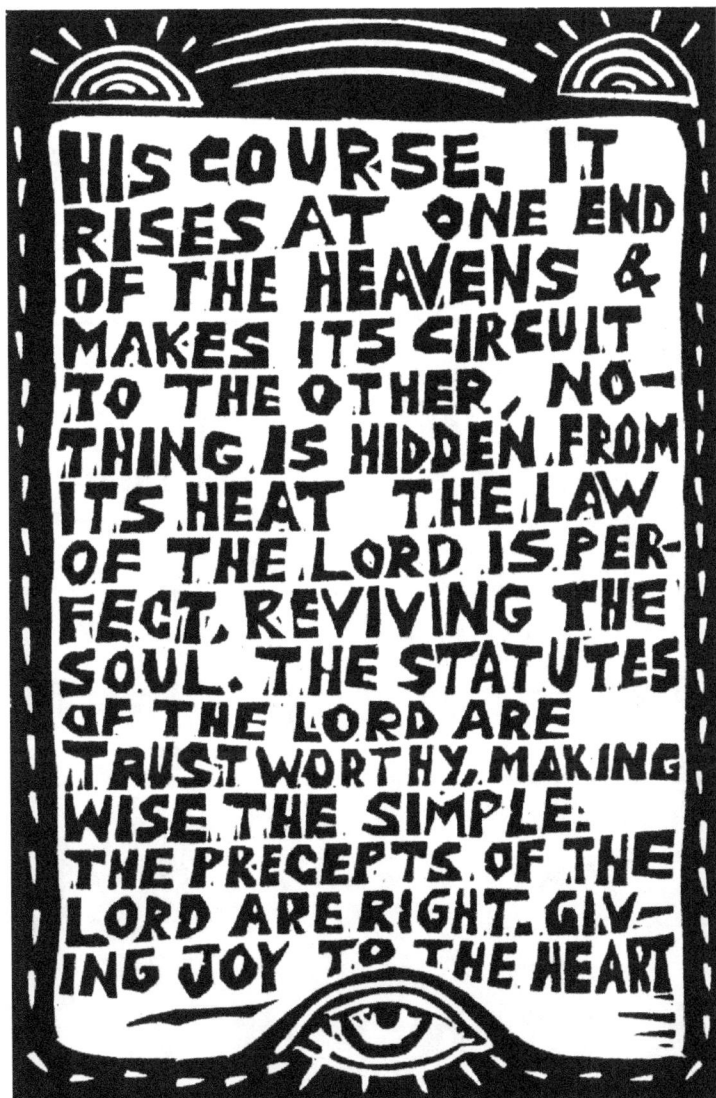

HIS COURSE. IT
RISES AT ONE END
OF THE HEAVENS &
MAKES ITS CIRCUIT
TO THE OTHER, NO-
THING IS HIDDEN FROM
ITS HEAT THE LAW
OF THE LORD IS PER-
FECT, REVIVING THE
SOUL. THE STATUTES
OF THE LORD ARE
TRUSTWORTHY, MAKING
WISE THE SIMPLE.
THE PRECEPTS OF THE
LORD ARE RIGHT. GIV-
ING JOY TO THE HEART

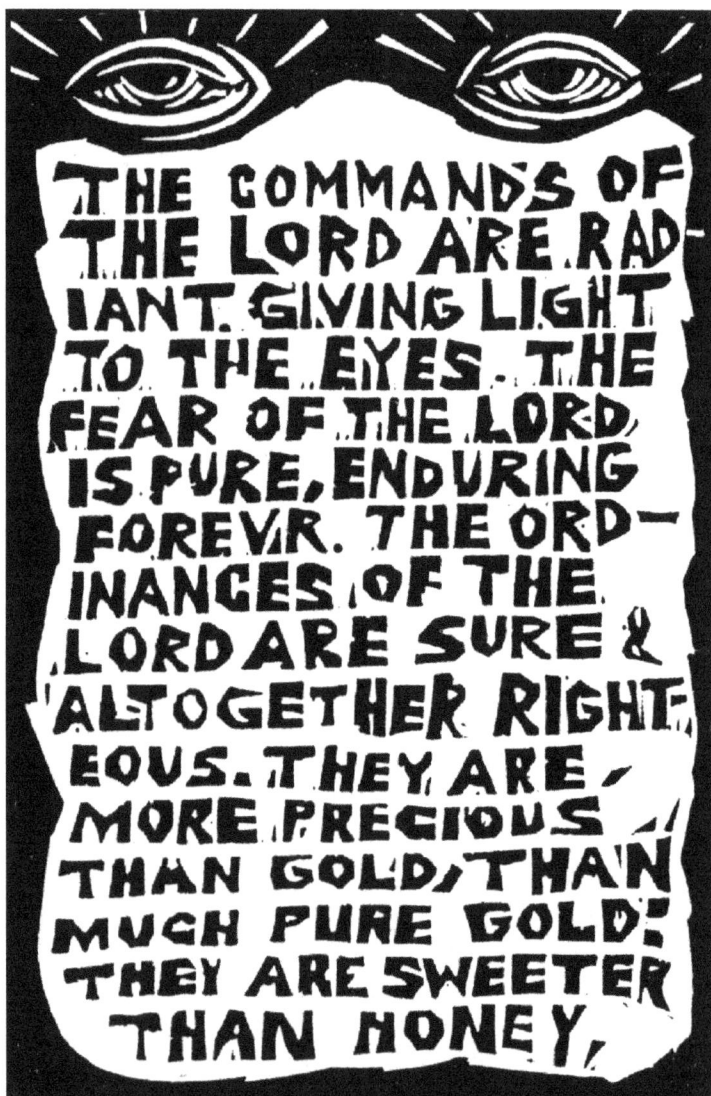

THE COMMANDS OF THE LORD ARE RADIANT. GIVING LIGHT TO THE EYES. THE FEAR OF THE LORD IS PURE, ENDURING FOREVR. THE ORDINANCES OF THE LORD ARE SURE & ALTOGETHER RIGHTEOUS. THEY ARE MORE PRECIOUS THAN GOLD, THAN MUCH PURE GOLD: THEY ARE SWEETER THAN HONEY,

THAN HONEY FROM THE COMB. BY THEM IS YOUR SERVANT WARNED; IN KEEPING THEM THERE IS GREAT REWARD. WHO CAN DISCERN HIS ERRORS? FORGIVE MY HIDDEN FAULTS. KEEP YOUR SERVANT ALSO FROM WILLFUL SINS; MAY THEY NOT RULE OVER ME

14

THE HEART OF JESUS

ST. BERNARD OF CLAIRVAUX

15

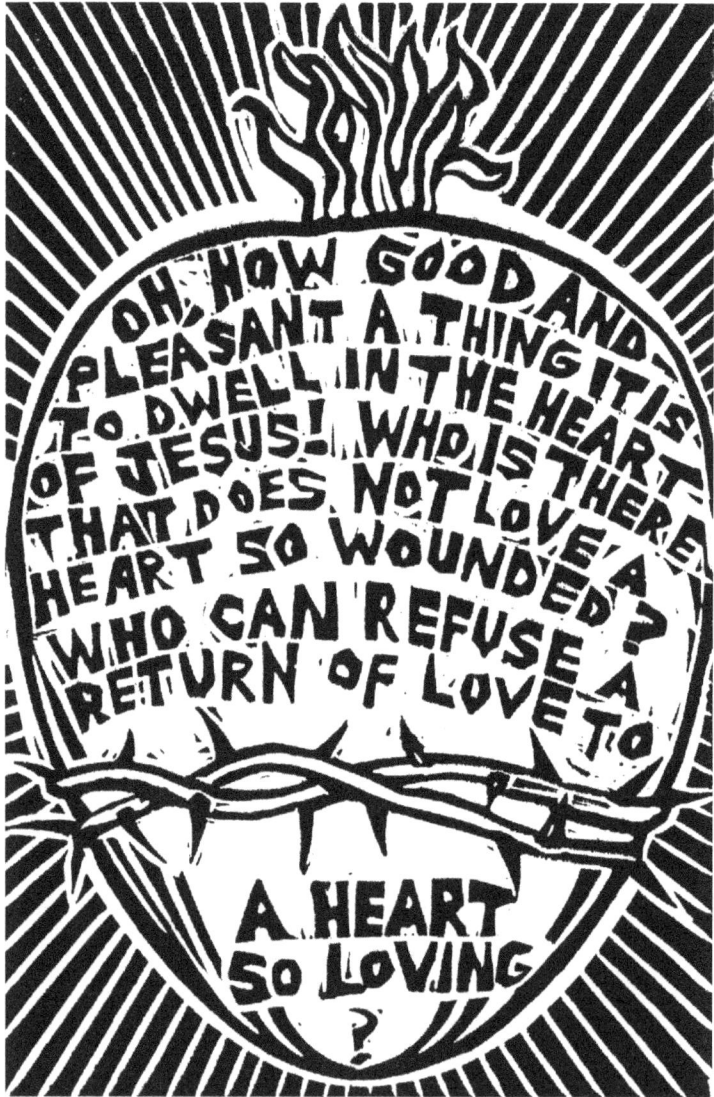

OH, HOW GOOD AND PLEASANT A THING IT IS TO DWELL IN THE HEART OF JESUS! WHO IS THERE THAT DOES NOT LOVE A HEART SO WOUNDED? WHO CAN REFUSE A RETURN OF LOVE TO A HEART SO LOVING?

Hope
is the
thing with
feathers
that perches in the
soul, and sings the tune
without the words,
and never stops at
all
and sweetest in the
gale is heard; and
sore must be the
storm that could
abash the little bird
that kept so
many warm.

i've heard it
in the chilliest
land and on the
strangest sea;
yet, never, in
    extremity,
it asked a
crumb
of
me.

SELAH

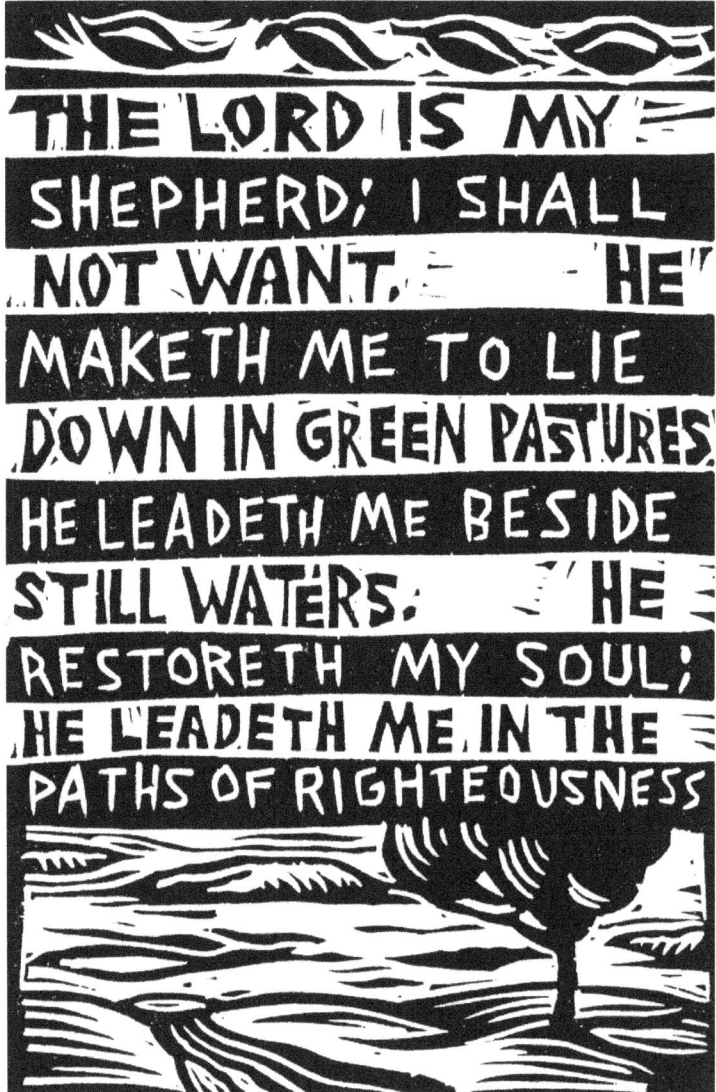

THE LORD IS MY SHEPHERD; I SHALL NOT WANT. HE MAKETH ME TO LIE DOWN IN GREEN PASTURES. HE LEADETH ME BESIDE STILL WATERS. HE RESTORETH MY SOUL; HE LEADETH ME IN THE PATHS OF RIGHTEOUSNESS

FOR HIS NAMES SAKE.
YEA, THOUGH I WALK
THROUGH THE VALLEY
OF THE SHADOW OF
DEATH, I WILL FEAR NO
EVIL: FOR THOU ART WITH
ME; THY ROD AND THY
STAFF THEY COMFORT
ME. THOU PREPAREST A
TABLE BEFORE ME IN
THE PRESENCE OF MINE
ENEMIES: THOU

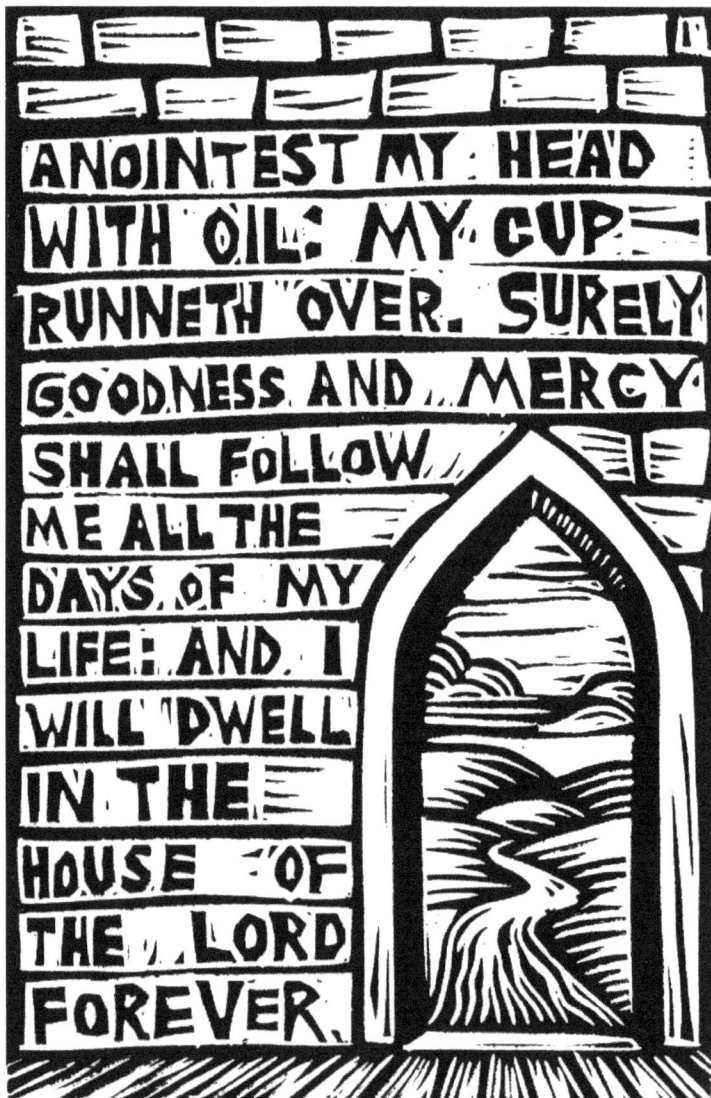

ANOINTEST MY HEAD WITH OIL: MY CUP RUNNETH OVER. SURELY GOODNESS AND MERCY SHALL FOLLOW ME ALL THE DAYS OF MY LIFE: AND I WILL DWELL IN THE HOUSE OF THE LORD FOREVER.

MY MOST SWEET LORD
I OFFER AND CONSECRATE
TO YOU THIS MORNING ALL
THAT I AM AND HAVE:
MY SENSES, MY
THOUGHTS, MY AF-
FECTIONS, MY DESIRES
MY PLEASURES, MY
INCLINATIONS, MY
LIBERTY.
IN A WORD, I
PLACE MY
WHOLE BODY
AND SOUL IN YOUR
HANDS

26

COME MY LIGHT

DIMITRII OF ROSTOV

COME, MY LIGHT, & ILLUMINE MY DARK-
NESS. COME, MY LIFE, & REVIVE ME
FROM DEATH. COME, MY PHYSICIAN, &
HEAL MY WOUNDS. COME, FLAME OF DI-
VINE LOVE, & BURN UP THE THORNS OF MY SINS, KINDLING MY HEART
WITH THE FLAME OF YOUR LOVE. COME
MY KING, SIT UPON THE THRONE OF MY
HEART & REIGN THERE.

FOR YOU
ALONE
ARE MY
KING &
MY
LORD.

PRAISE GOD IN HIS SANCTUARY; PRAISE HIM IN HIS MIGHTY HEAVENS. PRAISE

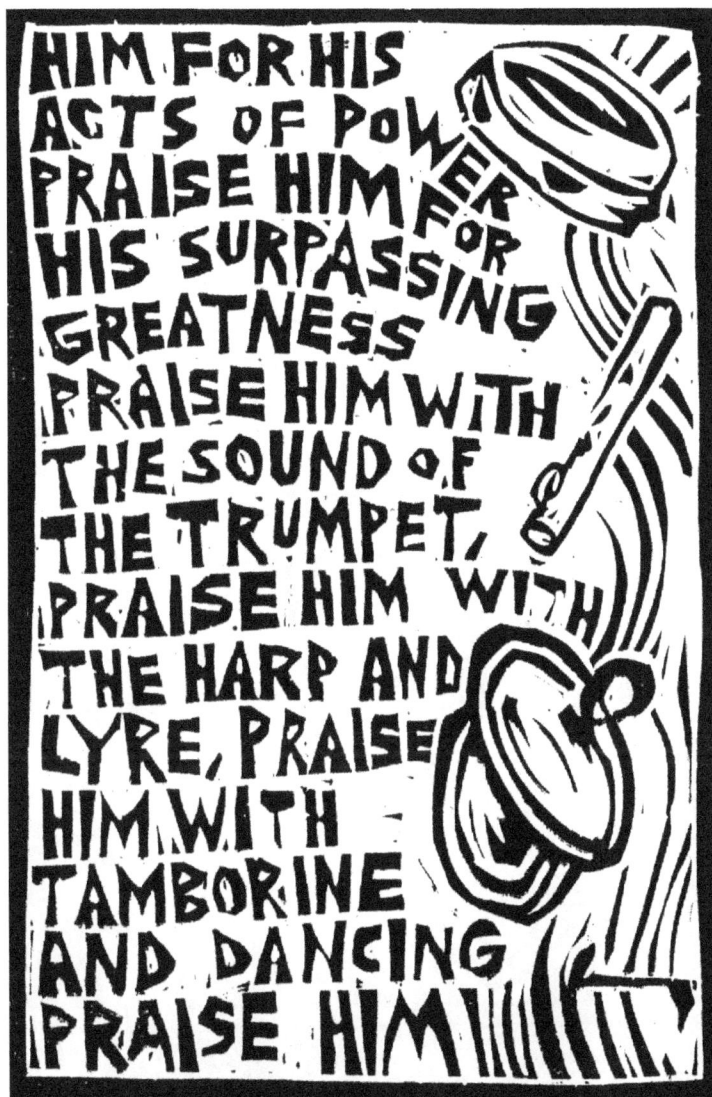

HIM FOR HIS ACTS OF POWER PRAISE HIM FOR HIS SURPASSING GREATNESS PRAISE HIM WITH THE SOUND OF THE TRUMPET, PRAISE HIM WITH THE HARP AND LYRE, PRAISE HIM WITH TAMBORINE AND DANCING PRAISE HIM

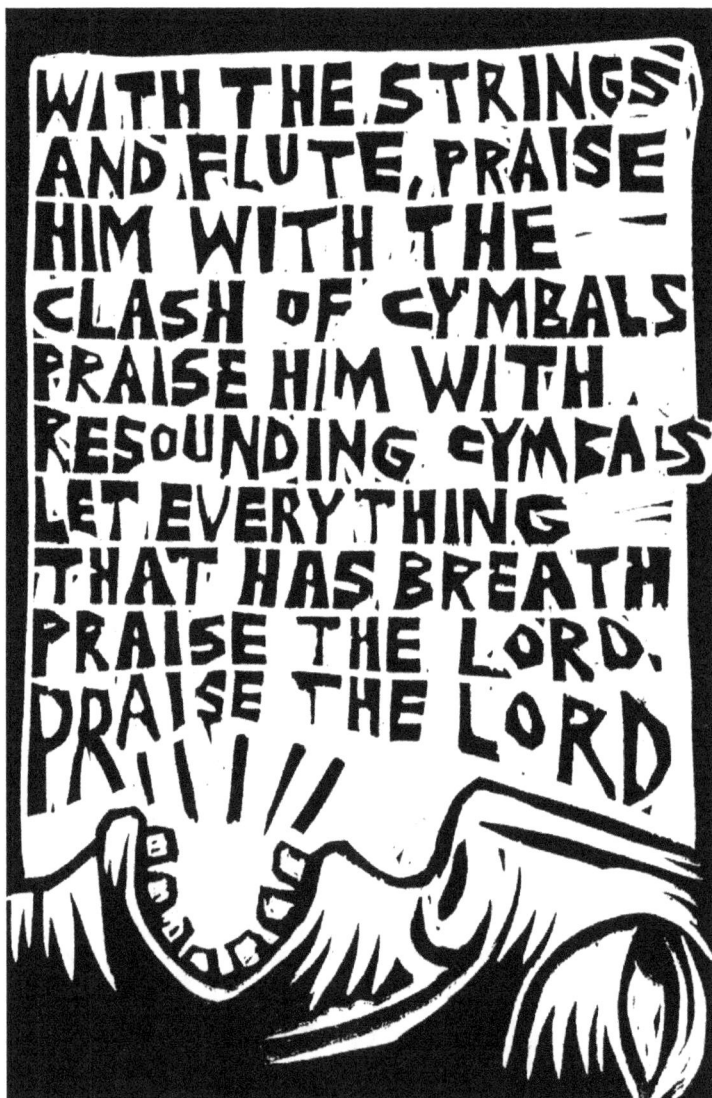

WITH THE STRINGS
AND FLUTE, PRAISE
HIM WITH THE
CLASH OF CYMBALS
PRAISE HIM WITH
RESOUNDING CYMBALS
LET EVERYTHING
THAT HAS BREATH
PRAISE THE LORD,
PRAISE THE LORD

LORD, MAKE ME AN INSTRUMENT OF YOUR PEACE. WHERE THERE IS HATRED, LET ME SOW LOVE. WHERE THERE IS INJURY PARDON. WHERE THERE IS DOUBT, FAITH. WHERE THERE IS DESPAIR HOPE. WHERE THERE IS DARKNESS, LIGHT, AND WHERE THERE IS SADNESS, JOY.

O DIVINE MASTER GRANT THAT I MAY

NOT SO MUCH SEEK TO BE CONSOLED AS TO CONSOLE; TO BE UNDERSTOOD AS TO UNDERSTAND; TO BE LOVED AS TO LOVE; FOR IT IS IN GIVING THAT WE RECEIVE, IT IS IN PARDONING THAT WE ARE PARDONED, AND IT IS IN DYING THAT WE ARE BORN TO ETERNAL LIFE

SELAH

11

THE BRANCH

HILDEGARD
OF
BINGEN

o budded greening branch! You stand firmly rooted in your mobility As the dawn advances. Now rejoice & be glad; consider us frail ones worthy To free us from our destructive ways Put forth your hand & raise us up.

38

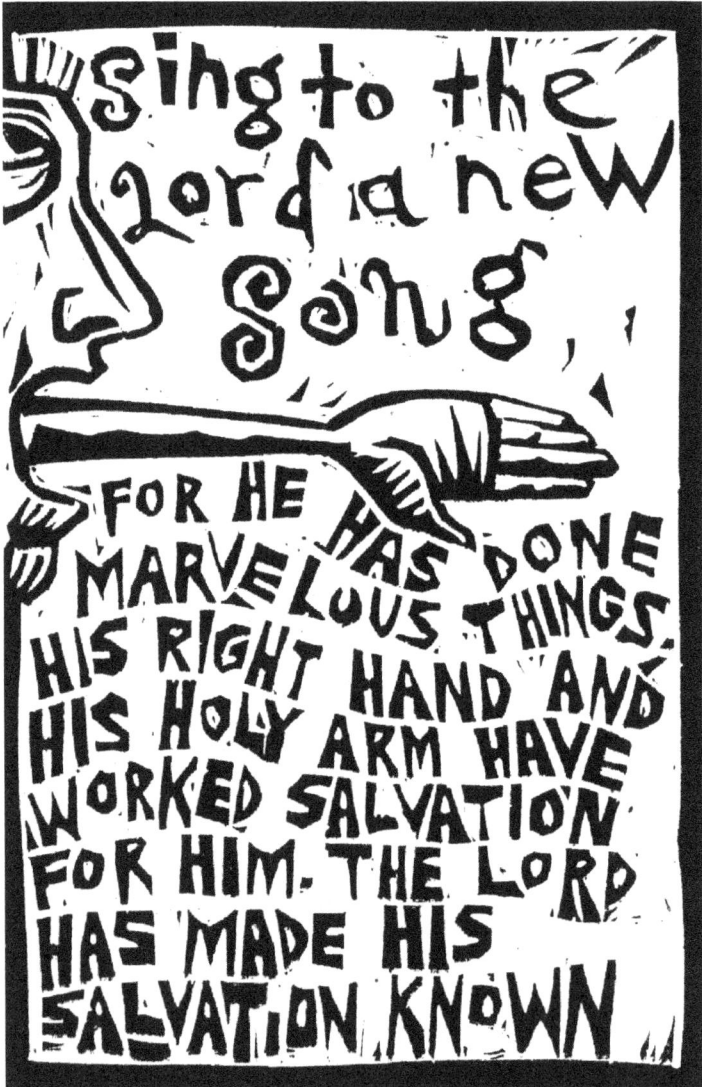

Sing to the Lord a new song, for he has done marvelous things. His right hand and his holy arm have worked salvation for him. The Lord has made his salvation known

40

AND
REVEALED
HIS RIGHTEOUS-
NESS TO THE NA-
TIONS. HE HAS RE-
MEMBERED HIS LOVE
AND HIS FAITHFUL-
NESS TO THE
HOUSE OF ISRAEL,
ALL THE ENDS OF
THE EARTH HAVE
SEEN THE SALVA-
TION OF OUR GOD.
SHOUT FOR JOY TO
THE LORD, ALL THE

*EARTH, BURST INTO JUBILANT SONG WITH MUSIC; MAKE MUSIC TO THE LORD WITH THE HARP; WITH THE HARP AND THE SOUND OF SINGING, WITH * TRUMPETS AND THE

BLAST OF THE RAM'S
HORN—SHOUT FOR
JOY BEFORE THE
LORD, THE KING. LET
THE SEA RESOUND
AND EVERYTHING IN
IT, THE WORLD AND
ALL WHO LIVE IN IT.
LET THE RIVERS CLAP
THEIR HANDS,

LET THE MOUNT-AINS SING FOR JOY; LET THEM SING BEFORE THE LORD, FOR HE COMES TO JUDGE THE EARTH, HE WILL JUDGE THE WORLD IN RIGHT-EOUSNESS AND THE PEOPLES WITH EQUITY

LET NOTHING DISTURB YOU, NOTHING FRIGHTEN YOU, ALL THINGS ARE PASSING, PATIENT ENDURANCE ATTAINS ALL THINGS: ONE WHO GOD POSSESSES WANTS NOTHING FOR GOD ALONE SUFFICES

14

PRAYER OF SURRENDER

IGNATIUS OF LOYOLA

RECIEVE, LORD, all my LIBERTY, my memory, my UNDERSTANDING, & MY WHOLE WILL, YOU HAVE GIVEN ME ALL THAT I HAVE, ALL THAT I AM. & I SURRENDER ALL TO YOUR DIVINE WILL, THAT YOU DISPOSE OF ME. GIVE ME only your love & your GRACE. WITH THIS I AM RICH ENOUGH, & HAVE NO MORE TO ASK.

PRAISE THE LORD. PRAISE THE LORD, O MY SOUL. I WILL PRAISE THE LORD ALL MY LIFE: I WILL SING PRAISE TO MY GOD AS LONG AS I LIVE DO NOT PUT YOUR TRUST IN PRINCES IN MORTAL MEN WHO CANNOT SAVE. WHEN THEIR SPIRIT DEPARTS, THEY RETURN TO THE GROUND ON THAT VERY DAY THEIR

PLANS COME TO NOTHING BLESSED IS HE WHOSE HELP IS THE GOD OF JACOB, WHOSE HOPE IS IN THE LORD HIS GOD THE MAKER OF HEAVEN AND EARTH THE SEA AND EVERYTHING IN THEM =

THE LORD, WHO RE-MAINS FAITHFUL FOR-EVER, HE UPHOLDS THE CAUSE OF THE OPPRESSED AND GIVES FOOD TO THE HUNGRY. THE LORD SETS

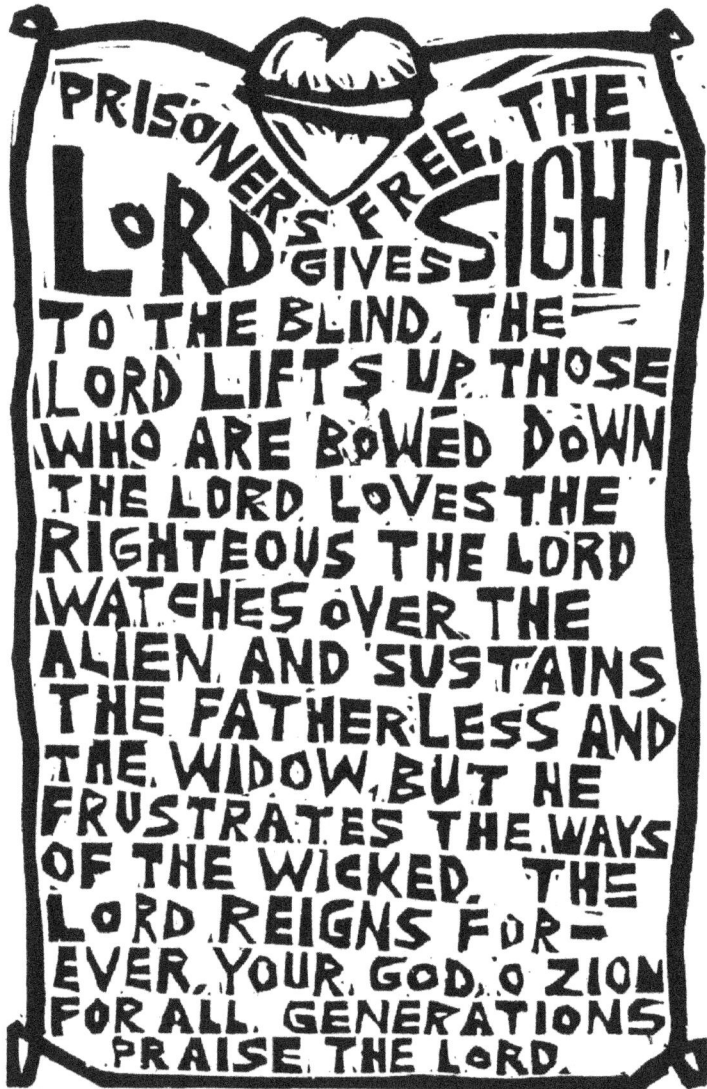

PRISONERS FREE, THE LORD GIVES SIGHT TO THE BLIND, THE LORD LIFTS UP THOSE WHO ARE BOWED DOWN THE LORD LOVES THE RIGHTEOUS THE LORD WATCHES OVER THE ALIEN, AND SUSTAINS THE FATHERLESS AND THE WIDOW, BUT HE FRUSTRATES THE WAYS OF THE WICKED. THE LORD REIGNS FOR-EVER, YOUR GOD, O ZION FOR ALL GENERATIONS PRAISE THE LORD.

I HAVE ONLY TODAY

THERESE OF LISIEUX

MY LIFE IS AN INSTANT
AN HOUR WHICH PASSES BY: MY LIFE IS A MOMENT WHICH I HAVE NO POWER TO STAY YOU KNOW O MY GOD THAT TO LOVE YOU HERE ON EARTH
I HAVE ONLY TODAY

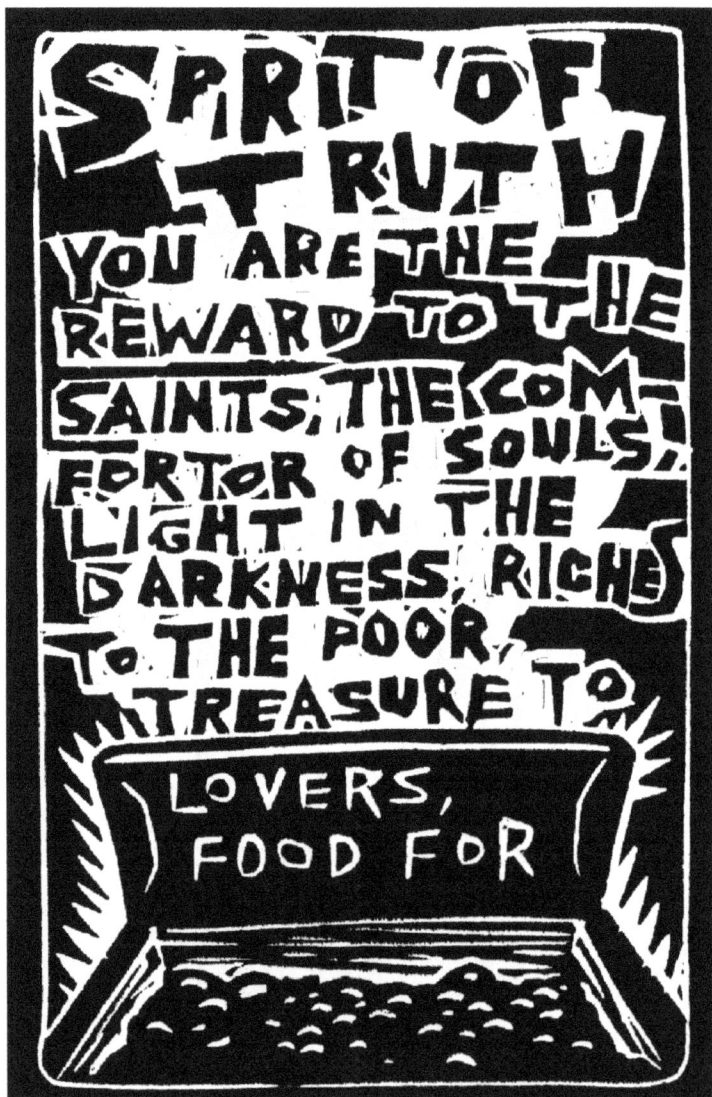

SPIRIT OF TRUTH YOU ARE THE REWARD TO THE SAINTS, THE COMFORTER OF SOULS, LIGHT IN THE DARKNESS, RICHES TO THE POOR, TREASURE TO LOVERS, FOOD FOR

THE HUNGRY, COMFORT TO THE WANDERER TO SUM UP, YOU ARE THE ONE IN WHOM ALL TREASURES ARE CONTAINED

57

SELAH

18

PSALM
113

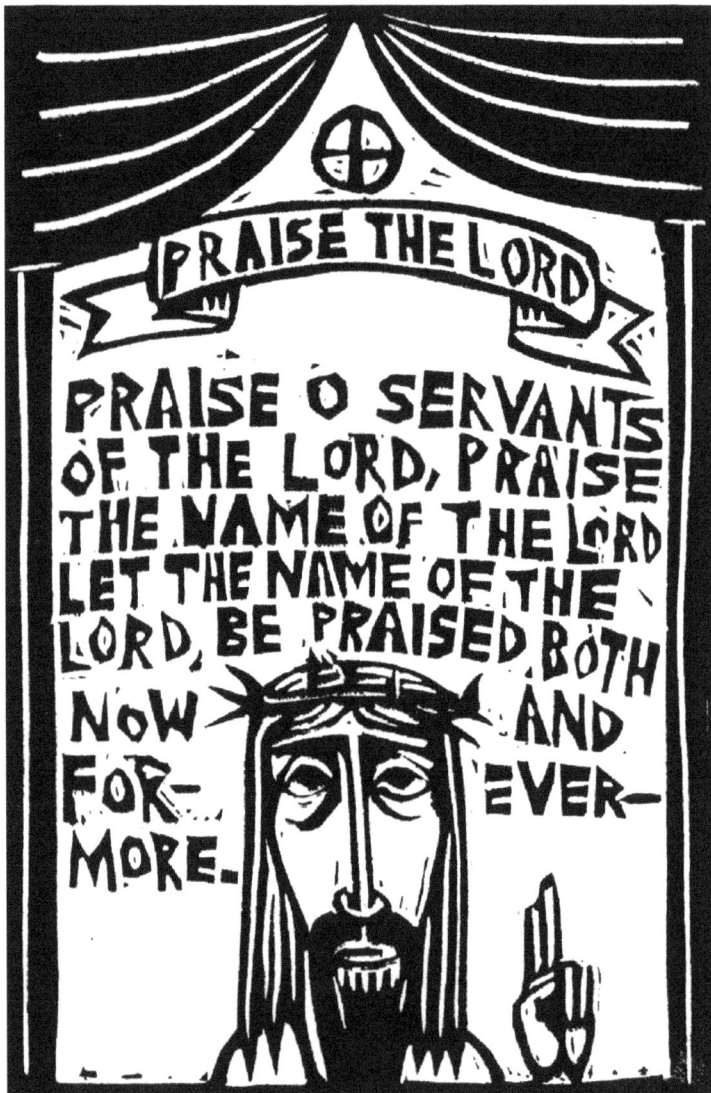

PRAISE THE LORD

PRAISE O SERVANTS OF THE LORD, PRAISE THE NAME OF THE LORD LET THE NAME OF THE LORD, BE PRAISED BOTH NOW AND FOR-MORE. EVER-

FROM THE RISING TO BE PRAISED. OF THE SUN TO THE PLACE WHERE IT SETS, THE NAME OF THE LORD IS TO BE PRAISED. THE LORD IS EXALTED OVER ALL THE NATIONS, HIS GLORY ABOVE THE HEAVENS. WHO IS LIKE THE LORD OUR GOD, THE ONE WHO SITS ENTHRONED ON HIGH,

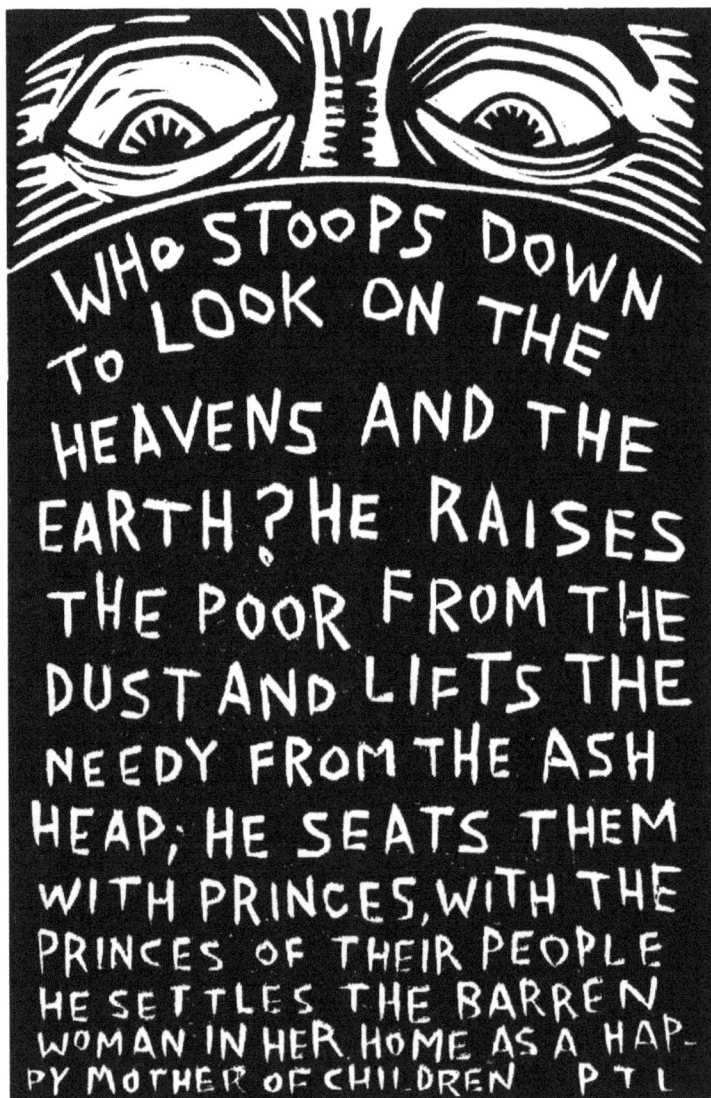

WHO STOOPS DOWN TO LOOK ON THE HEAVENS AND THE EARTH? HE RAISES THE POOR FROM THE DUST AND LIFTS THE NEEDY FROM THE ASH HEAP; HE SEATS THEM WITH PRINCES, WITH THE PRINCES OF THEIR PEOPLE HE SETTLES THE BARREN WOMAN IN HER HOME AS A HAPPY MOTHER OF CHILDREN   PTL

GO FORTH IN PEACE, FOR YOU HAVE FOLLOWED THE GOOD ROAD. GO FORTH WITHOUT FEAR FOR HE WHO CREATED YOU HAS MADE YOU HOLY, HAS ALWAYS PROTECTED YOU, AND LOVES YOU AS A MOTHER.

BLESSED BE YOU, MY GOD, FOR HAVING CREATED ME.

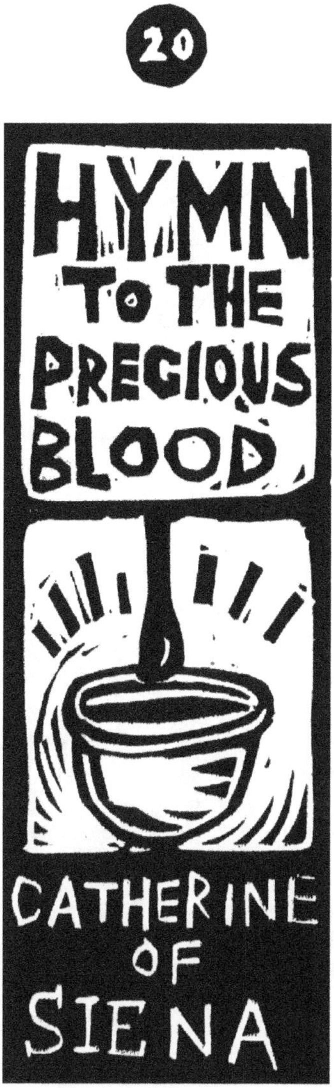

20

HYMN TO THE PRECIOUS BLOOD

CATHERINE OF SIENA

PRECIOUS BLOOD, OCEAN OF DIVINE MERCY: FLOW UPON US! PRECIOUS BLOOD, MOST

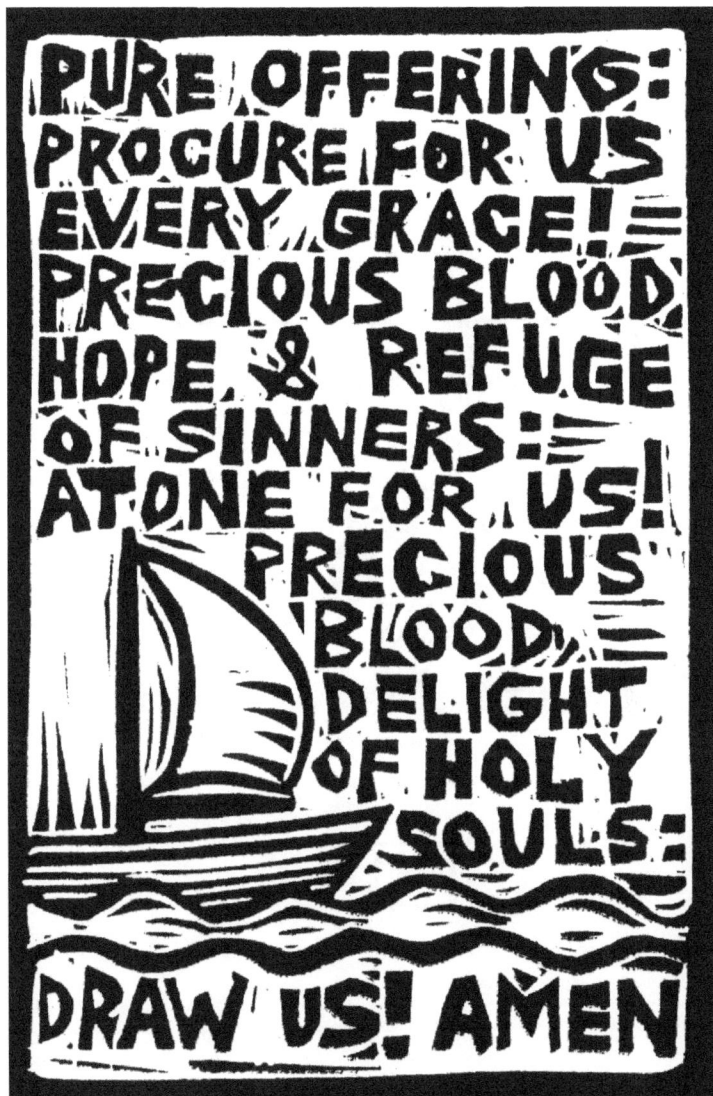

PURE OFFERING:
PROCURE FOR US
EVERY GRACE!
PRECIOUS BLOOD
HOPE & REFUGE
OF SINNERS:
ATONE FOR US!
PRECIOUS
BLOOD,
DELIGHT
OF HOLY
SOULS:
DRAW US! AMEN

SELAH

PRAISE THE LORD ALL YOU SERVANTS OF THE LORD WHO MINISTER BY NIGHT IN THE HOUSE OF THE LORD, LIFT UP YOUR HANDS IN THE SANCTUARY

SELAH

72

22

A QUIET CHAMBER

MARTIN LUTHER

OH, DEAREST
JESUS, HOLY
CHILD MAKE
THEE A BED,
SOFT,
UNDEFILED,
WITHIN
MY
HEART
THAT IT MAY
BE A QUIET
CHAMBER KEPT
FOR THEE.

23

GRATITUDE

ST. RICHARD OF CHICHESTER

THANK YOU, LORD JESUS CHRIST FOR ALL THE BENEFITS AND BLESSINGS WHICH YOU HAVE GIVEN ME,

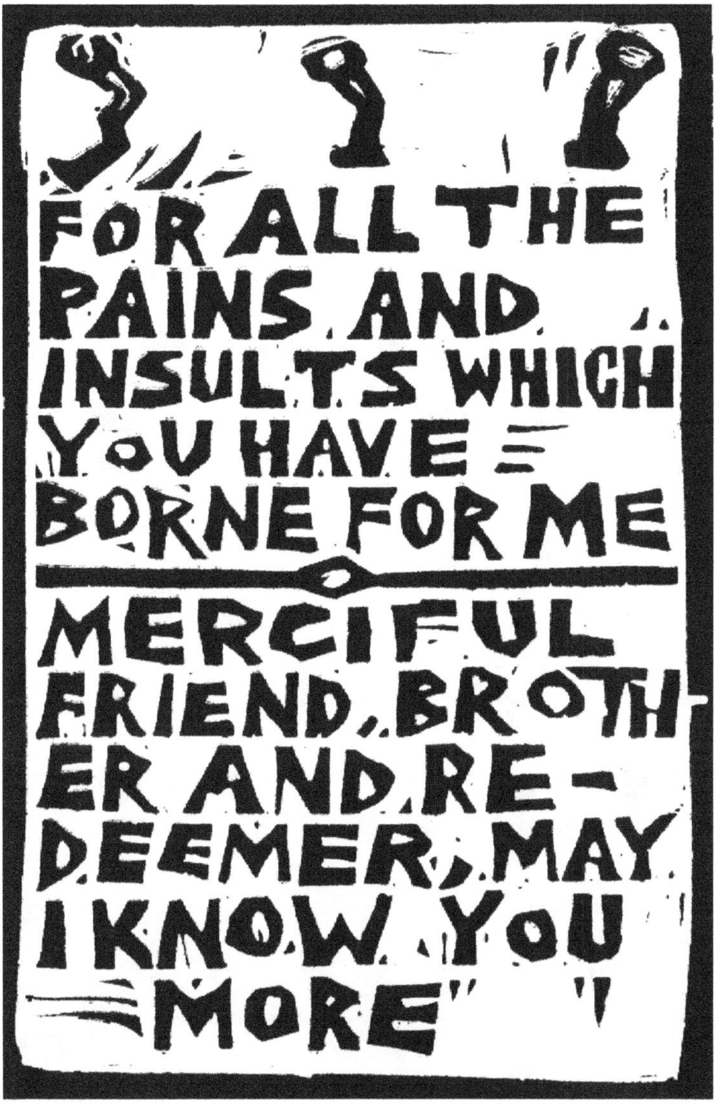

"FOR ALL THE PAINS AND INSULTS WHICH YOU HAVE BORNE FOR ME MERCIFUL FRIEND, BROTHER AND REDEEMER, MAY I KNOW YOU MORE"

CLEARLY,
LOVE YOU
MORE
DEARLY, AND
FOLLOW
YOU MORE
NEARLY
DAY BY DAY

When the Lord brought back the captives to Zion we were like men who dreamed. Our mouths were filled with laughter, our tongues with songs of joy.

80

THEN IT WAS SAID AMONG THE NATIONS THE LORD HAS DONE GREAT THINGS FOR THEM. THE LORD HAS DONE GREAT THINGS FOR US, AND WE ARE FILLED WITH JOY. RESTORE OUR FORTUNES, O LORD, LIKE STREAMS IN THE NEGEV. THOSE WHO SOW IN TEARS

WILL REAP WITH SONGS OF JOY HE WHO GOES OUT WEEPING, CARRYING SEED TO SOW, WILL RETURN WITH SONGS OF JOY, CARRYING SHEAVES WITH HIM.

O LORD MY GOD
TEACH MY HEART
THIS DAY WHERE
AND HOW TO SEE
YOU, WHERE AND
HOW TO FIND YOU
YOU HAVE MADE
ME AND REMADE
ME AND YOU
HAVE

BESTOWED ON ME
ALL THE GOOD
THINGS I POSSESS
AND STILL I DO
NOT KNOW YOU.
I HAVE NOT YET
DONE THAT FOR
WHICH I WAS MADE
TEACH ME TO SEEK
FOR I CANNOT SEEK
UNLESS YOU TEACH
ME, OR FIND YOU
UNLESS YOU SHOW

YOURSELF TO ME. LET ME SEEK YOU IN MY DESIRE, LET ME DESIRE YOU IN MY SEEK-ING, LET ME FIND YOU BY LOVING YOU, LET ME LOVE YOU WHEN I FIND YOU.

26

I HAVE BUT THEE

CHRISTINA ROSSETTI

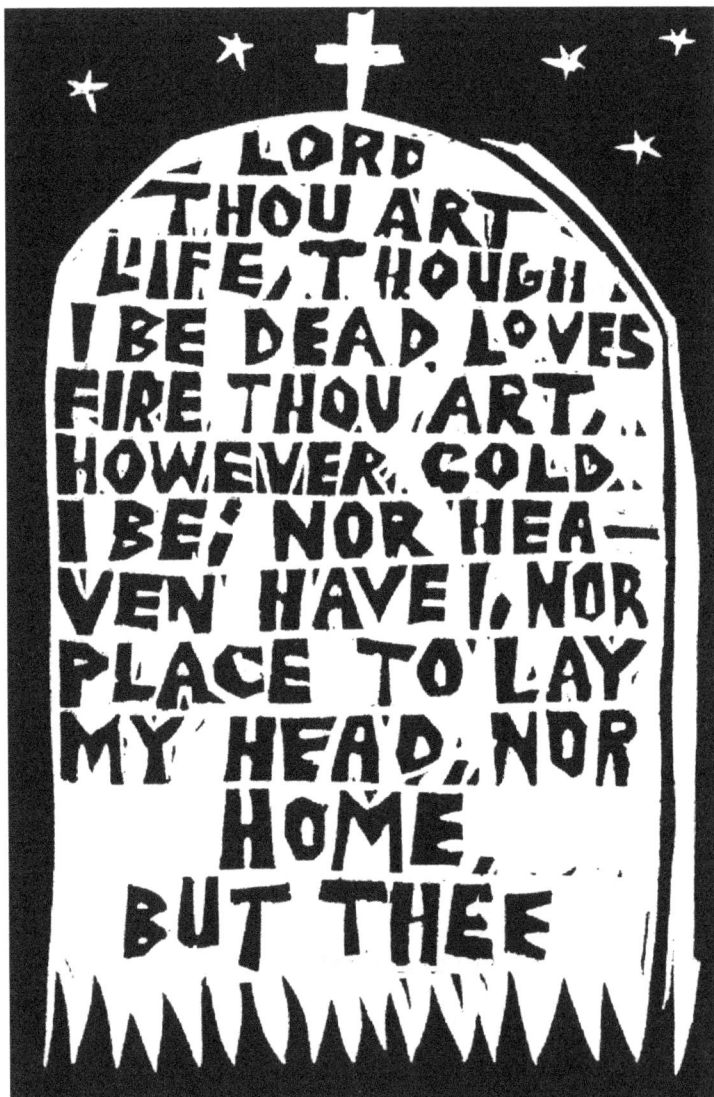

LORD
THOU ART
LIFE, THOUGH
I BE DEAD. LOVES
FIRE THOU ART,
HOWEVER COLD
I BE; NOR HEA—
VEN HAVE I, NOR
PLACE TO LAY
MY HEAD, NOR
HOME,
BUT THEE

OUT OF THE DEPTHS I CRY TO YOU, O LORD; O LORD, HEAR MY VOICE. LET YOUR EARS BE ATTENTIVE TO MY CRY FOR MERCY. IF YOU KEPT A RECORD OF SINS, O LORD WHO COULD STAND? BUT WITH YOU THERE IS FORGIVENESS; THEREFORE YOU ARE FEARED. I WAIT FOR THE LORD,

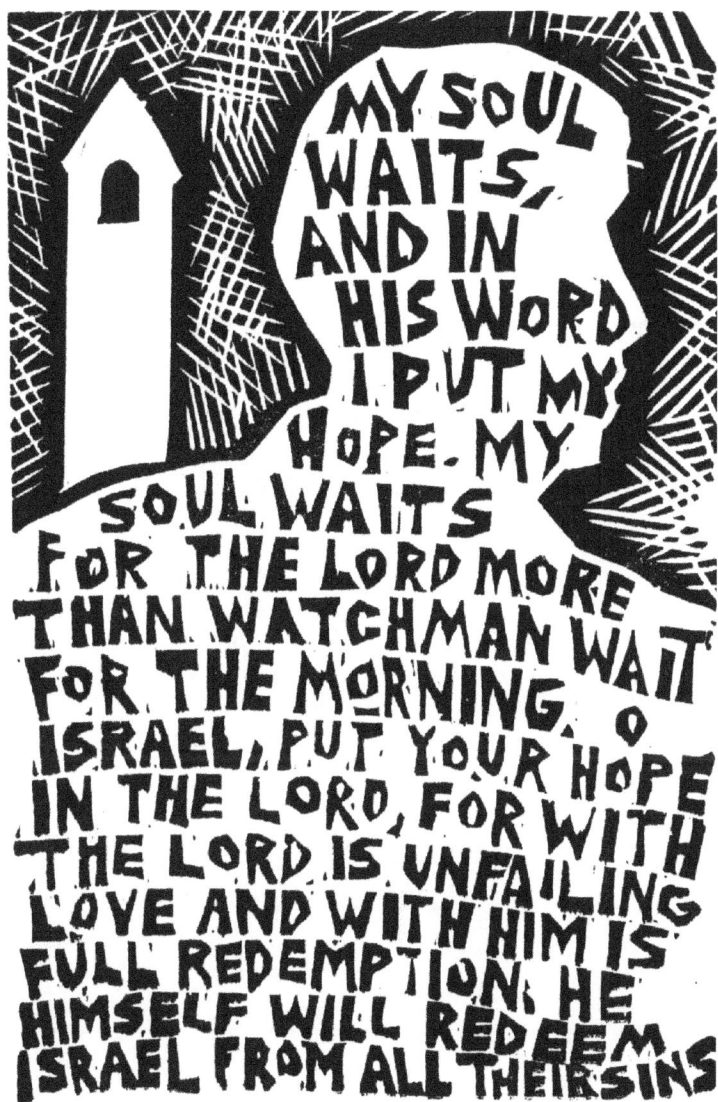

MY SOUL WAITS, AND IN HIS WORD I PUT MY HOPE. MY SOUL WAITS FOR THE LORD MORE THAN WATCHMAN WAIT FOR THE MORNING. O ISRAEL, PUT YOUR HOPE IN THE LORD, FOR WITH THE LORD IS UNFAILING LOVE AND WITH HIM IS FULL REDEMPTION. HE HIMSELF WILL REDEEM ISRAEL FROM ALL THEIR SINS

SELAH

28

DESIRE OF A DEVOUT BELIEVER

BENEDICT OF NURSIA

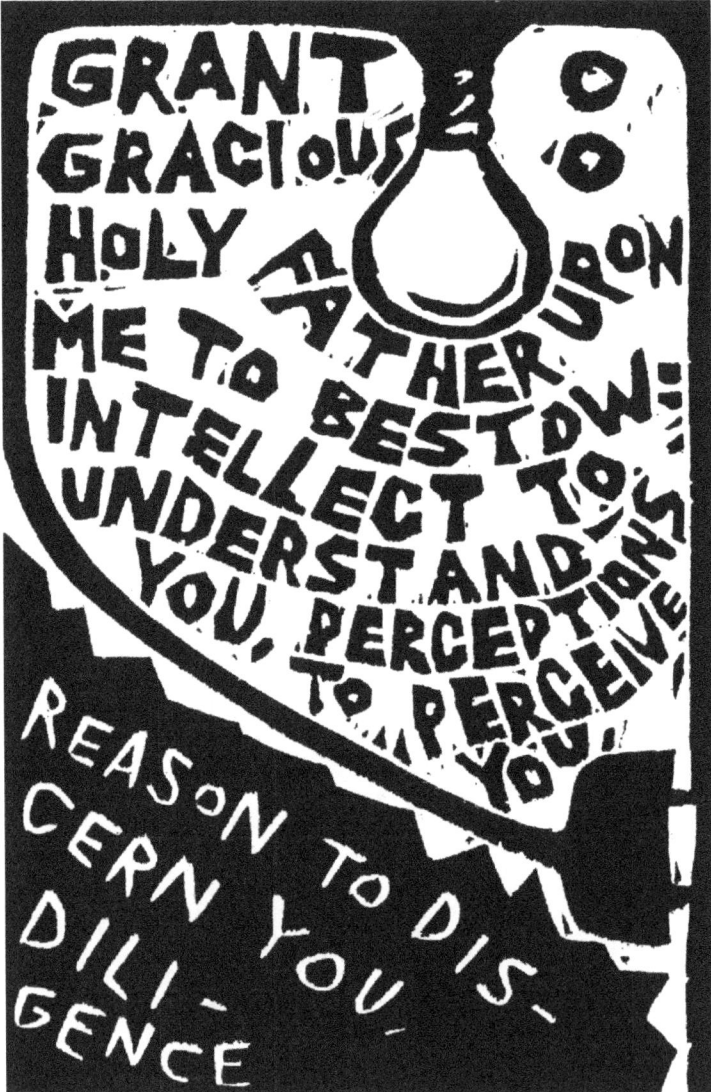

GRANT, O GRACIOUS HOLY FATHER UPON ME TO BESTOW: INTELLECT TO UNDERSTAND YOU, PERCEPTIONS TO PERCEIVE YOU, REASON TO DIS-CERN YOU, DILI-GENCE

TO SEEK YOU, WISDOM TO FIND YOU, A SPIRIT TO KNOW YOU.

SELAH

FOR LIGHT
IN DARK
TIMES

ST.
AUGUSTINE

GOD OF LIFE, THERE ARE DAYS WHEN THE BURDENS WE CARRY

CHAFE OUR SHOULDERS & WEAR US DOWN WHEN THE ROAD SEEMS DREARY & ENDLESS, THE SKIES GRAY & THREAT-ENING; WHEN OUR LIVES HAVE NO MUSIC IN THEM & OUR HEARTS ARE LONELY

AND OUR
SOULS HAVE
LOST THEIR
COURAGE. FLOOD
THE PATH WITH
LIGHT WE BE-
SEACH YOU; TURN
OUR EYES
TO WHERE
THE SKIES
ARE FULL
OF PROM-
ISE.

30

GLORY INTO GLORY

CHARLES WESLEY

FINISH, THEN, THY
NEW CREATION;
PURE AND SPOTLESS
LET US BE, LET US
SEE THY GREAT SAL-
VATION PERFECTLY
RESTORED IN THEE;
CHANGED FROM GLORY
INTO GLORY, TILL IN
HEAVEN WE TAKE OUR
PLACE, TILL WE CAST
OUR CROWNS BEFORE
THEE, LOST IN WON-
DER, LOVE & PRAISE

ETERNAL LIGHT,
SHINE INTO OUR
HEARTS; ETERNAL
GOODNESS, DELIVER
US FROM EVIL
ETERNAL POW-
ER, BE OUR SUP-
PORT; ETERNAL
WISDOM, SCATTER
THE DARKNESS OF OUR
IGNORANCE; ETERNAL
PITY, HAVE MERCY ON
US — SO THAT WITH
ALL OUR HEART AND
MIND AND SOUL AND
STRENGTH WE MAY
SEEK YOUR

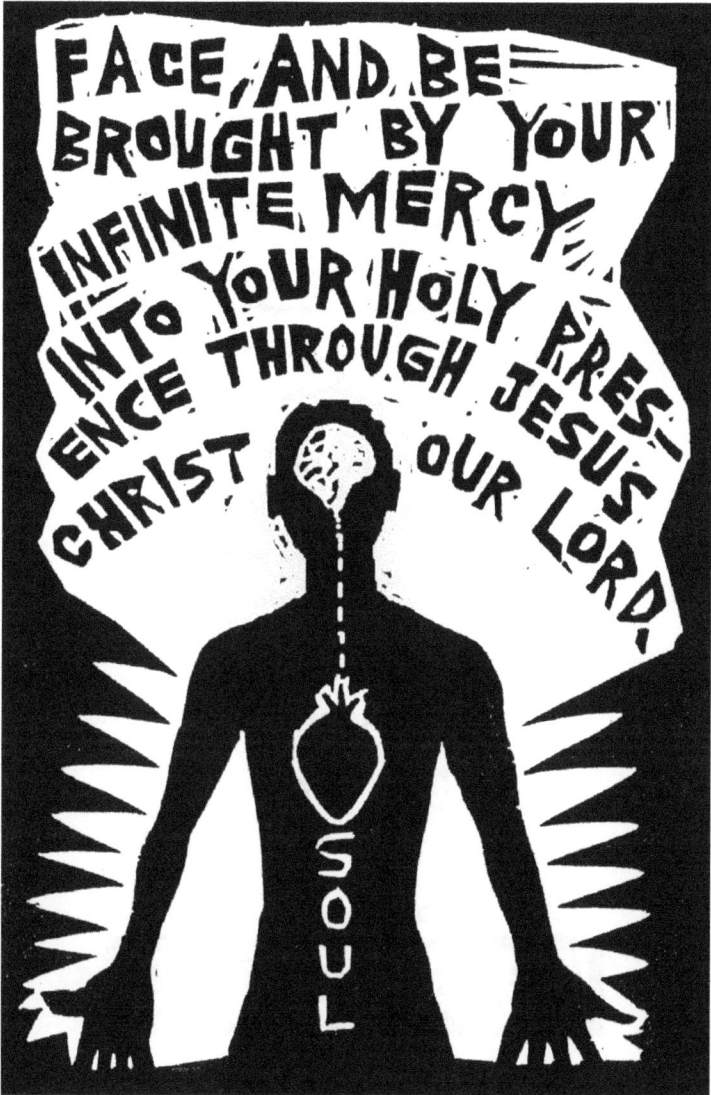

ABOUT THE ARTIST

I RECEIVED MY MA FROM EASTERN
ILLINOIS UNIVERSITY, AND MY BA
FROM TRINITY U. IN SAN ANTONIO.
INITIALLY TRAINED AS A PAINTER,
I TOOK AN INTEREST IN BLOCKPRINTS
AROUND 1994 AND HAVE BEEN DOING
THEM EVER SINCE.
HAVING TAUGHT ART FOR 13 YEARS,
I BECAME A FULL TIME ARTIST
IN 2003. I NOW SELL MY ART
THROUGH ART FAIRS, GALLERIES,
AND MY WEBSITE.

STARVING
ARTIST
B O O K S

ALL PROFITS FROM THIS BOOK ARE
DONATED TO VARIOUS CHARITIES.

www.ingramcontent.com/pod-product-compliance
Lightning Source LLC
Chambersburg PA
CBHW021342090426
42742CB00008B/708